HAL•LEONARD

JAZZ PLAY-ALONG®

ook and CD for B♭, E♭, C and Bass Clef Instruments

volume
171

Arranged by **Mark Taylor**
Produced by **Jim Roberts,**
Craig Fraedrich,
and Paul Murtha

RADIOH...
10 GREAT SONGS

BOOK

CD

ISBN 978-1-4768-6795-3

HAL•LEONARD®
CORPORATION

7777 W. BLUEMOUND RD. P.O. BOX 13819 MILWAUKEE, WI 53213

In Australia Contact:
Hal Leonard Australia Pty. Ltd.
4 Lentara Court
Cheltenham, Victoria, 3192 Australia
Email: ausadmin@halleonard.com.au

Visit Hal Leonard Online at
www.halleonard.com

RADIOHEAD

Volume 171

Arranged by Mark Taylor
Produced by Jim Roberts, Craig Fraedrich, and Paul Murtha

Featured Players:

Graham Breedlove–Trumpet
John Desalme–Tenor Sax and Clarinet
Tony Nalker–Piano
Jim Roberts–Guitar
Paul Henry–Bass
Todd Harrison–Drums

**Recorded at Bias Studios, Springfield, Virginia
Bob Dawson, Engineer**

HOW TO USE THE CD:
Each song has <u>two</u> tracks:

1) Split Track/Melody

Woodwind, Brass, Keyboard, and **Mallet Players** can use this track as a learning tool for melody style and inflection.

Bass Players can learn and perform with this track – remove the recorded bass track by turning down the volume on the LEFT channel.

Keyboard and **Guitar Players** can learn and perform with this track – remove the recorded piano part by turning down the volume on the RIGHT channel.

2) Full Stereo Track

Soloists or **Groups** can learn and perform with this accompaniment track with the RHYTHM SECTION only.

CREEP

WORDS AND MUSIC BY ALBERT HAMMOND,
MIKE HAZLEWOOD, THOMAS YORKE,
JONATHAN GREENWOOD, COLIN GREENWOOD,
EDWARD O'BRIEN AND PHILIP SELWAY

C VERSION

5

CD
◆ 3 : SPLIT TRACK/MELODY
◆ 4 : FULL STEREO TRACK

C VERSION

EVERYTHING IN ITS RIGHT PLACE

WORDS AND MUSIC BY THOMAS YORKE,
JONATHAN GREENWOOD, COLIN GREENWOOD,
EDWARD O'BRIEN AND PHILIP SELWAY

MY IRON LUNG

WORDS AND MUSIC BY THOMAS YORKE,
JONATHAN GREENWOOD, COLIN GREENWOOD,
EDWARD O'BRIEN AND PHILIP SELWAY

C VERSION

EXIT MUSIC
(FOR A FILM)

WORDS AND MUSIC BY THOMAS YORKE,
JONATHAN GREENWOOD, COLIN GREENWOOD,
EDWARD O'BRIEN AND PHILIP SELWAY

C VERSION

MOLTO RIT.

HIGH AND DRY

WORDS AND MUSIC BY THOMAS YORKE,
JONATHAN GREENWOOD, COLIN GREENWOOD,
EDWARD O'BRIEN AND PHILIP SELWAY

C VERSION

KNIVES OUT

WORDS AND MUSIC BY THOMAS YORKE,
JONATHAN GREENWOOD, COLIN GREENWOOD,
EDWARD O'BRIEN AND PHILIP SELWAY

C VERSION

13

OPTIMISTIC

WORDS AND MUSIC BY THOMAS YORKE,
JONATHAN GREENWOOD, COLIN GREENWOOD,
EDWARD O'BRIEN AND PHILIP SELWAY

C VERSION

PARANOID ANDROID

CD
15 : SPLIT TRACK/MELODY
16 : FULL STEREO TRACK

WORDS AND MUSIC BY THOMAS YORKE,
JONATHAN GREENWOOD, COLIN GREENWOOD,
EDWARD O'BRIEN AND PHILIP SELWAY

C VERSION

CD

17 : SPLIT TRACK/MELODY
18 : FULL STEREO TRACK

C VERSION

PYRAMID SONG

WORDS AND MUSIC BY THOMAS YORKE,
JONATHAN GREENWOOD, COLIN GREENWOOD,
EDWARD O'BRIEN AND PHILIP SELWAY

SUBTERRANEAN HOMESICK ALIEN

CD
19 : SPLIT TRACK/MELODY
20 : FULL STEREO TRACK

C VERSION

WORDS AND MUSIC BY THOMAS YORKE,
JONATHAN GREENWOOD, COLIN GREENWOOD,
EDWARD O'BRIEN AND PHILIP SELWAY

CREEP

WORDS AND MUSIC BY ALBERT HAMMOND,
MIKE HAZLEWOOD, THOMAS YORKE,
JONATHAN GREENWOOD, COLIN GREENWOOD,
EDWARD O'BRIEN AND PHILIP SELWAY

EVERYTHING IN ITS RIGHT PLACE

WORDS AND MUSIC BY THOMAS YORKE,
JONATHAN GREENWOOD, COLIN GREENWOOD,
EDWARD O'BRIEN AND PHILIP SELWAY

Bb VERSION

MY IRON LUNG

CD
11 : SPLIT TRACK/MELODY
12 : FULL STEREO TRACK

Bb VERSION

WORDS AND MUSIC BY THOMAS YORKE,
JONATHAN GREENWOOD, COLIN GREENWOOD,
EDWARD O'BRIEN AND PHILIP SELWAY

CD
5: SPLIT TRACK/MELODY
6: FULL STEREO TRACK

Bb VERSION

EXIT MUSIC
(FOR A FILM)

WORDS AND MUSIC BY THOMAS YORKE,
JONATHAN GREENWOOD, COLIN GREENWOOD,
EDWARD O'BRIEN AND PHILIP SELWAY

MOLTO RIT.

HIGH AND DRY

WORDS AND MUSIC BY THOMAS YORKE,
JONATHAN GREENWOOD, COLIN GREENWOOD,
EDWARD O'BRIEN AND PHILIP SELWAY

CD

7 : SPLIT TRACK/MELODY
8 : FULL STEREO TRACK

Bb VERSION

KNIVES OUT

WORDS AND MUSIC BY THOMAS YORKE,
JONATHAN GREENWOOD, COLIN GREENWOOD,
EDWARD O'BRIEN AND PHILIP SELWAY

Bb VERSION

OPTIMISTIC

WORDS AND MUSIC BY THOMAS YORKE,
JONATHAN GREENWOOD, COLIN GREENWOOD,
EDWARD O'BRIEN AND PHILIP SELWAY

Bb VERSION

PARANOID ANDROID

WORDS AND MUSIC BY THOMAS YORKE,
JONATHAN GREENWOOD, COLIN GREENWOOD,
EDWARD O'BRIEN AND PHILIP SELWAY

Bb VERSION

CD
17 : SPLIT TRACK/MELODY
18 : FULL STEREO TRACK

Bb VERSION

PYRAMID SONG

WORDS AND MUSIC BY THOMAS YORKE,
JONATHAN GREENWOOD, COLIN GREENWOOD,
EDWARD O'BRIEN AND PHILIP SELWAY

SUBTERRANEAN HOMESICK ALIEN

CD
19 : SPLIT TRACK/MELODY
20 : FULL STEREO TRACK

Bb VERSION

WORDS AND MUSIC BY THOMAS YORKE,
JONATHAN GREENWOOD, COLIN GREENWOOD,
EDWARD O'BRIEN AND PHILIP SELWAY

CREEP

WORDS AND MUSIC BY ALBERT HAMMOND,
MIKE HAZLEWOOD, THOMAS YORKE,
JONATHAN GREENWOOD, COLIN GREENWOOD,
EDWARD O'BRIEN AND PHILIP SELWAY

Eb VERSION

CD
3 : Split Track/Melody
4 : Full Stereo Track

Eb Version

EVERYTHING IN ITS RIGHT PLACE

WORDS AND MUSIC BY THOMAS YORKE,
JONATHAN GREENWOOD, COLIN GREENWOOD,
EDWARD O'BRIEN AND PHILIP SELWAY

MY IRON LUNG

WORDS AND MUSIC BY THOMAS YORKE,
JONATHAN GREENWOOD, COLIN GREENWOOD,
EDWARD O'BRIEN AND PHILIP SELWAY

CD

11 : SPLIT TRACK/MELODY

12 : FULL STEREO TRACK

Eb VERSION

EXIT MUSIC
(FOR A FILM)

Eb VERSION

WORDS AND MUSIC BY THOMAS YORKE,
JONATHAN GREENWOOD, COLIN GREENWOOD,
EDWARD O'BRIEN AND PHILIP SELWAY

SLOW ROCK BALLAD

MOLTO RIT.

HIGH AND DRY

WORDS AND MUSIC BY THOMAS YORKE, JONATHAN GREENWOOD, COLIN GREENWOOD, EDWARD O'BRIEN AND PHILIP SELWAY

CD

7: SPLIT TRACK/MELODY
8: FULL STEREO TRACK

Eb VERSION

KNIVES OUT

WORDS AND MUSIC BY THOMAS YORKE,
JONATHAN GREENWOOD, COLIN GREENWOOD,
EDWARD O'BRIEN AND PHILIP SELWAY

Eb VERSION

OPTIMISTIC

WORDS AND MUSIC BY THOMAS YORKE,
JONATHAN GREENWOOD, COLIN GREENWOOD,
EDWARD O'BRIEN AND PHILIP SELWAY

CD

🔷13 : SPLIT TRACK/MELODY
🔷14 : FULL STEREO TRACK

Eb VERSION

PARANOID ANDROID

WORDS AND MUSIC BY THOMAS YORKE,
JONATHAN GREENWOOD, COLIN GREENWOOD,
EDWARD O'BRIEN AND PHILIP SELWAY

Eb VERSION

Pyramid Song

WORDS AND MUSIC BY THOMAS YORKE,
JONATHAN GREENWOOD, COLIN GREENWOOD,
EDWARD O'BRIEN AND PHILIP SELWAY

Eb VERSION

SUBTERRANEAN HOMESICK ALIEN

CD
19 : SPLIT TRACK/MELODY
20 : FULL STEREO TRACK

Eb VERSION

WORDS AND MUSIC BY THOMAS YORKE,
JONATHAN GREENWOOD, COLIN GREENWOOD,
EDWARD O'BRIEN AND PHILIP SELWAY

CREEP

WORDS AND MUSIC BY ALBERT HAMMOND,
MIKE HAZLEWOOD, THOMAS YORKE,
JONATHAN GREENWOOD, COLIN GREENWOOD,
EDWARD O'BRIEN AND PHILIP SELWAY

EVERYTHING IN ITS RIGHT PLACE

WORDS AND MUSIC BY THOMAS YORKE,
JONATHAN GREENWOOD, COLIN GREENWOOD,
EDWARD O'BRIEN AND PHILIP SELWAY

🎼: C VERSION

MY IRON LUNG

WORDS AND MUSIC BY THOMAS YORKE,
JONATHAN GREENWOOD, COLIN GREENWOOD,
EDWARD O'BRIEN AND PHILIP SELWAY

EXIT MUSIC
(FOR A FILM)

WORDS AND MUSIC BY THOMAS YORKE,
JONATHAN GREENWOOD, COLIN GREENWOOD,
EDWARD O'BRIEN AND PHILIP SELWAY

MOLTO RIT.

HIGH AND DRY

WORDS AND MUSIC BY THOMAS YORKE,
JONATHAN GREENWOOD, COLIN GREENWOOD,
EDWARD O'BRIEN AND PHILIP SELWAY

KNIVES OUT

WORDS AND MUSIC BY THOMAS YORKE,
JONATHAN GREENWOOD, COLIN GREENWOOD,
EDWARD O'BRIEN AND PHILIP SELWAY

OPTIMISTIC

WORDS AND MUSIC BY THOMAS YORKE,
JONATHAN GREENWOOD, COLIN GREENWOOD,
EDWARD O'BRIEN AND PHILIP SELWAY

PARANOID ANDROID

WORDS AND MUSIC BY THOMAS YORKE,
JONATHAN GREENWOOD, COLIN GREENWOOD,
EDWARD O'BRIEN AND PHILIP SELWAY

17 : SPLIT TRACK/MELODY
18 : FULL STEREO TRACK

𝄢 : C VERSION

PYRAMID SONG

WORDS AND MUSIC BY THOMAS YORKE,
JONATHAN GREENWOOD, COLIN GREENWOOD,
EDWARD O'BRIEN AND PHILIP SELWAY

SUBTERRANEAN HOMESICK ALIEN

WORDS AND MUSIC BY THOMAS YORKE,
JONATHAN GREENWOOD, COLIN GREENWOOD,
EDWARD O'BRIEN AND PHILIP SELWAY

CD
19 : SPLIT TRACK/MELODY
20 : FULL STEREO TRACK

C VERSION

MEDIUM JAZZ WALTZ

Presenting the Hal Leonard JAZZ PLAY-ALONG® SERIES

For use with all B-flat, E-flat, Bass Clef and C instruments, the Jazz Play-Along® Series is the ultimate learning tool for all jazz musicians. With musician-friendly lead sheets, melody cues, and other split-track choices on the included CD, these first-of-a-kind packages help you master improvisation while playing some of the greatest tunes of all time. FOR STUDY, each tune includes a split track with: melody cue with proper style and inflection • professional rhythm tracks • choruses for soloing • removable bass part • removable piano part. FOR PERFORMANCE, each tune also has: an additional full stereo accompaniment track (no melody) • additional choruses for soloing.

73. **JAZZ/BLUES**
   00843075......................................$14.95

74. **BEST JAZZ CLASSICS**
   00843076......................................$15.99

75. **PAUL DESMOND**
   00843077......................................$16.99

76. **BROADWAY JAZZ BALLADS**
   00843078......................................$15.99

77. **JAZZ ON BROADWAY**
   00843079......................................$15.99

78. **STEELY DAN**
   00843070......................................$15.99

79. **MILES DAVIS CLASSICS**
   00843081......................................$15.99

80. **JIMI HENDRIX**
   00843083......................................$16.99

81. **FRANK SINATRA – CLASSICS**
   00843084......................................$15.99

82. **FRANK SINATRA – STANDARDS**
   00843085......................................$16.99

83. **ANDREW LLOYD WEBBER**
   00843104......................................$14.95

84. **BOSSA NOVA CLASSICS**
   00843105......................................$14.95

85. **MOTOWN HITS**
   00843109......................................$14.95

86. **BENNY GOODMAN**
   00843110......................................$15.99

87. **DIXIELAND**
   00843111......................................$16.99

88. **DUKE ELLINGTON FAVORITES**
   00843112......................................$14.95

89. **IRVING BERLIN FAVORITES**
   00843113......................................$14.95

90. **THELONIOUS MONK CLASSICS**
   00841262......................................$16.99

91. **THELONIOUS MONK FAVORITES**
   00841263......................................$16.99

92. **LEONARD BERNSTEIN**
   00450134......................................$15.99

93. **DISNEY FAVORITES**
   00843142......................................$14.99

94. **RAY**
   00843143......................................$14.99

95. **JAZZ AT THE LOUNGE**
   00843144......................................$14.99

96. **LATIN JAZZ STANDARDS**
   00843145......................................$15.99

97. **MAYBE I'M AMAZED***
   00843148......................................$15.99

98. **DAVE FRISHBERG**
   00843149......................................$15.99

99. **SWINGING STANDARDS**
   00843150......................................$14.99

100. **LOUIS ARMSTRONG**
   00740423......................................$16.99

101. **BUD POWELL**
   00843152......................................$14.99

102. **JAZZ POP**
   00843153......................................$15.99

103. **ON GREEN DOLPHIN STREET
   & OTHER JAZZ CLASSICS**
   00843154......................................$14.99

104. **ELTON JOHN**
   00843155......................................$14.99

105. **SOULFUL JAZZ**
   00843151......................................$15.99

106. **SLO' JAZZ**
   00843117......................................$14.99

107. **MOTOWN CLASSICS**
   00843116......................................$14.99

108. **JAZZ WALTZ**
   00843159......................................$15.99

109. **OSCAR PETERSON**
   00843160......................................$16.99

110. **JUST STANDARDS**
   00843161......................................$15.99

111. **COOL CHRISTMAS**
   00843162......................................$15.99

112. **PAQUITO D'RIVERA – LATIN JAZZ***
   48020662......................................$16.99

113. **PAQUITO D'RIVERA – BRAZILIAN JAZZ***
   48020663......................................$19.99

114. **MODERN JAZZ QUARTET FAVORITES**
   00843163......................................$15.99

115. **THE SOUND OF MUSIC**
   00843164......................................$15.99

116. **JACO PASTORIUS**
   00843165......................................$15.99

117. **ANTONIO CARLOS JOBIM – MORE HITS**
   00843166......................................$15.99

118. **BIG JAZZ STANDARDS COLLECTION**
   00843167......................................$27.50

119. **JELLY ROLL MORTON**
   00843168......................................$15.99

120. **J.S. BACH**
   00843169......................................$15.99

121. **DJANGO REINHARDT**
   00843170......................................$15.99

122. **PAUL SIMON**
   00843182......................................$16.99

123. **BACHARACH & DAVID**
   00843185......................................$15.99

124. **JAZZ-ROCK HORN HITS**
   00843186......................................$15.99

126. **COUNT BASIE CLASSICS**
   00843157......................................$15.99

127. **CHUCK MANGIONE**
   00843188......................................$15.99

128. **VOCAL STANDARDS (LOW VOICE)**
   00843189......................................$15.99

129. **VOCAL STANDARDS (HIGH VOICE)**
   00843190......................................$15.99

130. **VOCAL JAZZ (LOW VOICE)**
   00843191......................................$15.99

131. **VOCAL JAZZ (HIGH VOICE)**
   00843192......................................$15.99

132. **STAN GETZ ESSENTIALS**
   00843193......................................$15.99

133. **STAN GETZ FAVORITES**
   00843194......................................$15.99

134. **NURSERY RHYMES***
   00843196......................................$17.99

135. **JEFF BECK**
   00843197......................................$15.99

136. **NAT ADDERLEY**
   00843198......................................$15.99

137. **WES MONTGOMERY**
   00843199......................................$15.99

138. **FREDDIE HUBBARD**
   00843200......................................$15.99

139. **JULIAN "CANNONBALL" ADDERLEY**
   00843201......................................$15.99

140. **JOE ZAWINUL**
   00843202......................................$15.99

141. **BILL EVANS STANDARDS**
   00843156......................................$15.99

142. **CHARLIE PARKER GEMS**
   00843222......................................$15.99

143. **JUST THE BLUES**
   00843223......................................$15.99

144. **LEE MORGAN**
   00843229......................................$15.99

145. **COUNTRY STANDARDS**
   00843230......................................$15.99

146. **RAMSEY LEWIS**
   00843231 ....$15.99

147. **SAMBA**
   00843232......................................$15.99

150. **JAZZ IMPROV BASICS**
   00843195......................................$19.99

151. **MODERN JAZZ QUARTET CLASSICS**
   00843209......................................$15.99

152. **J.J. JOHNSON**
   00843210......................................$15.99

154. **HENRY MANCINI**
   00843213......................................$14.99

155. **SMOOTH JAZZ CLASSICS**
   00843215......................................$15.99

156. **THELONIOUS MONK – EARLY GEMS**
   00843216......................................$15.99

157. **HYMNS**
   00843217......................................$15.99

158. **JAZZ COVERS ROCK**
   00843219......................................$15.99

159. **MOZART**
   00843220......................................$15.99

160. **GEORGE SHEARING**
   14041531......................................$16.99

161. **DAVE BRUBECK**
   14041556 ....$16.99

162. **BIG CHRISTMAS COLLECTION**
   00843221......................................$24.99

164. **HERB ALPERT**
   14041775 ....$16.99

165. **GEORGE BENSON**
   00843240......................................$16.99

167. **JOHNNY MANDEL**
   00103642......................................$16.99

168. **TADD DAMERON**
   00103663......................................$15.99

169. **BEST JAZZ STANDARDS**
   00109249......................................$19.99

170. **ULTIMATE JAZZ STANDARDS**
   00109250......................................$19.99

172. **POP STANDARDS**
   00111669......................................$15.99

174. **TIN PAN ALLEY**
   00119125......................................$15.99

175. **TANGO**
   00119836......................................$15.99

176. **JOHNNY MERCER**
   00119838......................................$15.99

*These CDs do not include split tracks.

Jazz Instruction & Improvisation

BOOKS FOR ALL INSTRUMENTS FROM HAL LEONARD

AN APPROACH TO JAZZ IMPROVISATION
by Dave Pozzi
Musicians Institute Press
Explore the styles of Charlie Parker, Sonny Rollins, Bud Powell and others with this comprehensive guide to jazz improvisation. Covers: scale choices • chord analysis • phrasing • melodies • harmonic progressions • more.
00695135 Book/CD Pack......................$17.95

THE ART OF MODULATING
FOR PIANISTS AND JAZZ MUSICIANS
by Carlos Salzedo &
Lucile Lawrence
Schirmer
The Art of Modulating is a treatise originally intended for the harp, but this edition has been edited for use by intermediate keyboardists and other musicians who have an understanding of basic music theory. In its pages you will find: table of intervals; modulation rules; modulation formulas; examples of modulation; extensions and cadences; ten fragments of dances; five characteristic pieces; and more.
50490581 ....$19.99

BUILDING A JAZZ VOCABULARY
By Mike Steinel
A valuable resource for learning the basics of jazz from Mike Steinel of the University of North Texas. It covers: the basics of jazz • how to build effective solos • a comprehensive practice routine • and a jazz vocabulary of the masters.
00849911 ....$19.95

THE CYCLE OF FIFTHS
by Emile and Laura De Cosmo
This essential instruction book provides more than 450 exercises, including hundreds of melodic and rhythmic ideas. The book is designed to help improvisors master the cycle of fifths, one of the primary progressions in music. Guaranteed to refine technique, enhance improvisational fluency, and improve sight-reading!
00311114 ....$16.99

THE DIATONIC CYCLE
by Emile and Laura De Cosmo
Renowned jazz educators Emile and Laura De Cosmo provide more than 300 exercises to help improvisors tackle one of music's most common progressions: the diatonic cycle. This book is guaranteed to refine technique, enhance improvisational fluency, and improve sight-reading!
00311115 ....$16.95

EAR TRAINING
by Keith Wyatt,
Carl Schroeder and Joe Elliott
Musicians Institute Press
Covers: basic pitch matching • singing major and minor scales • identifying intervals • transcribing melodies and rhythm • identifying chords and progressions • seventh chords and the blues • modal interchange, chromaticism, modulation • and more.
00695198 Book/2-CD Pack $24.95

EXERCISES AND ETUDES FOR THE JAZZ INSTRUMENTALIST
by J.J. Johnson
Designed as study material and playable by any instrument, these pieces run the gamut of the jazz experience, featuring common and uncommon time signatures and keys, and styles from ballads to funk. They are progressively graded so that both beginners and professionals will be challenged by the demands of this wonderful music.
00842018 Bass Clef Edition $16.95
00842042 Treble Clef Edition $16.95

JAZZOLOGY
THE ENCYCLOPEDIA OF JAZZ THEORY FOR ALL MUSICIANS
by Robert Rawlins and
Nor Eddine Bahha
This comprehensive resource covers a variety of jazz topics, for beginners and pros of any instrument. The book serves as an encyclopedia for reference, a thorough methodology for the student, and a workbook for the classroom.
00311167 ....$19.99

JAZZ THEORY RESOURCES
by Bert Ligon
Houston Publishing, Inc.
This is a jazz theory text in two volumes. **Volume 1 includes**: review of basic theory • rhythm in jazz performance • triadic generalization • diatonic harmonic progressions and analysis • substitutions and turnarounds • and more. **Volume 2 includes**: modes and modal frameworks • quartal harmony • extended tertian structures and triadic superimposition • pentatonic applications • coloring "outside" the lines and beyond • and more.
00030458 Volume 1 ....$39.95
00030459 Volume 2 ....$29.95

JOY OF IMPROV
by Dave Frank
and John Amaral
This book/CD course on improvisation for all instruments and all styles will help players develop monster musical skills! Book One imparts a solid basis in technique, rhythm, chord theory, ear training and improv concepts. **Book Two** explores more advanced chord voicings, chord arranging techniques and more challenging blues and melodic lines. The CD can be used as a listening and play-along tool.
00220005 Book 1 – Book/CD Pack......................$27.99
00220006 Book 2 – Book/CD Pack......................$26.99

THE PATH TO JAZZ IMPROVISATION
by Emile and Laura De Cosmo
This fascinating jazz instruction book offers an innovative, scholarly approach to the art of improvisation. It includes in-depth analysis and lessons about: cycle of fifths • diatonic cycle • overtone series • pentatonic scale • harmonic and melodic minor scale • polytonal order of keys • blues and bebop scales • modes • and more.
00310904 ....$14.99

THE SOURCE
THE DICTIONARY OF CONTEMPORARY AND TRADITIONAL SCALES
by Steve Barta
This book serves as an informative guide for people who are looking for good, solid information regarding scales, chords, and how they work together. It provides right and left hand fingerings for scales, chords, and complete inversions. Includes over 20 different scales, each written in all 12 keys.
00240885 ....$18.99

21 BEBOP EXERCISES
by Steve Rawlins
This book/CD pack is both a warm-up collection and a manual for bebop phrasing. Its tasty and sophisticated exercises will help you develop your proficiency with jazz interpretation. It concentrates on practice in all twelve keys – moving higher by half-step – to help develop dexterity and range. The companion CD includes all of the exercises in 12 keys.
00315341 Book/CD Pack....................$17.95

HAL•LEONARD® CORPORATION
7777 W. BLUEMOUND RD. P.O. BOX 13819 MILWAUKEE, WI 53213

Visit Hal Leonard online at
www.halleonard.com

Prices, contents & availability subject to change without notice.

0113

ARTIST TRANSCRIPTIONS

Artist Transcriptions are authentic, note-for-note transcriptions of today's hottest artists in jazz, pop and rock. These outstanding, accurate arrangements are in an easy-to-read format which includes all essential lines. **Artist Transcriptions** can be used to perform, sequence or for reference.

HAL•LEONARD® CORPORATION
7777 W. Bluemound Rd. P.O. Box 13819 Milwaukee, WI 53213

Visit our web site for a complete listing
of our titles with songlists at
www.halleonard.com

0913

Prices and availability subject to change without notice.

The Best-Selling Jazz Book of All Time Is Now Legal!

The Real Books are the most popular jazz books of all time. Since the 1970s, musicians have trusted these volumes to get them through every gig, night after night. The problem is that the books were illegally produced and distributed, without any regard to copyright law, or royalties paid to the composers who created these musical masterpieces.

Hal Leonard is very proud to present the first legitimate and legal editions of these books ever produced. You won't even notice the difference, other than all the notorious errors being fixed: the covers and typeface look the same, the song lists are nearly identical, and the price for our edition is even cheaper than the originals!

Every conscientious musician will appreciate that these books are now produced accurately and ethically, benefitting the songwriters that we owe for some of the greatest tunes of all time!

VOLUME 1

00240221	C Edition	$35.00
00240224	B♭ Edition	$35.00
00240225	E♭ Edition	$35.00
00240226	Bass Clef Edition	$35.00
00240292	C Edition 6 x 9	$30.00
00240339	B♭ Edition 6 x 9	$30.00
00451087	C Edition on CD-ROM	$25.00
00240302	A-D CD Backing Tracks	$24.99
00240303	E-J CD Backing Tracks	$24.95
00240304	L-R CD Backing Tracks	$24.95
00240305	S-Z CD Backing Tracks	$24.99
00110604	Book/USB Flash Drive Backing Tracks Pack	$79.99
00110599	USB Flash Drive Only	$50.00

VOLUME 2

00240222	C Edition	$35.50
00240227	B♭ Edition	$35.00
00240228	E♭ Edition	$35.00
00240229	Bass Clef Edition	$35.00
00240293	C Edition 6 x 9	$30.00
00451088	C Edition on CD-ROM	$27.99
00240351	A-D CD Backing Tracks	$24.99
00240352	E-I CD Backing Tracks	$24.99
00240353	J-R CD Backing Tracks	$24.99
00240354	S-Z CD Backing Tracks	$24.99

VOLUME 3

00240233	C Edition	$35.00
00240284	B♭ Edition	$35.00
00240285	E♭ Edition	$35.00
00240286	Bass Clef Edition	$35.00
00240338	C Edition 6 x 9	$30.00
00451089	C Edition on CD-ROM	$29.99

VOLUME 4

00240296	C Edition	$35.00
00103348	B♭ Edition	$35.00
00103349	E♭ Edition	$35.00
00103350	Bass Clef Edition	$35.00

VOLUME 5

00240349	C Edition	$35.00

Also available:

00240264	The Real Blues Book	$34.99
00310910	The Real Bluegrass Book	$29.99
00240137	Miles Davis Real Book	$19.95
00240355	The Real Dixieland Book	$29.99
00240235	The Duke Ellington Real Book	$19.99
00240348	The Real Latin Book	$35.00
00240358	The Charlie Parker Real Book	$19.99
00240331	The Bud Powell Real Book	$19.99
00240313	The Real Rock Book	$35.00
00240323	The Real Rock Book – Vol. 2	$35.00
00240359	The Real Tab Book – Vol. 1	$32.50
00240317	The Real Worship Book	$29.99

THE REAL CHRISTMAS BOOK

00240306	C Edition	$29.99
00240345	B♭ Edition	$29.99
00240346	E♭ Edition	$29.99
00240347	Bass Clef Edition	$29.99
00240431	A-G CD Backing Tracks	$24.99
00240432	H-M CD Backing Tracks	$24.99
00240433	N-Y CD Backing Tracks	$24.99

THE REAL VOCAL BOOK

00240230	Volume 1 High Voice	$35.00
00240307	Volume 1 Low Voice	$35.00
00240231	Volume 2 High Voice	$35.00
00240308	Volume 2 Low Voice	$35.00
00240391	Volume 3 High Voice	$35.00
00240392	Volume 3 Low Voice	$35.00

THE REAL BOOK – STAFF PAPER

00240327		$10.99

HOW TO PLAY FROM A REAL BOOK

FOR ALL MUSICIANS
by Robert Rawlins

00312097	$17.50

Complete song lists online at www.halleonard.com

Prices, content, and availability subject to change without notice.

HAL•LEONARD®
CORPORATION

7777 W. BLUEMOUND RD. P.O. BOX 13819 MILWAUKEE, WI 53213

1113